Dear Brother;

How I Praise
Your Deep Concern For Lost
Souls. May This Book Be
Helpful In Sharing Your
Faith With Them. God Bless
You As You Continue To Serve Him!

Daniel 12=3

11-7-09

Secret

to an

Open Door

Second Edition

David A. Morel

Secret to an Open Door

Second Edition

© 2002, 2005 David A. Morel

ISBN 0-9722152-1-2

ECPA: Evangelism / Outreach

Contact: GroupSource Travel
1-800-800-2519
www.davidmorel.net

TABLE OF CONTENTS

About the Author

David Morel served for more than 10 years at the world headquarters of one of the largest missionary outreach ministries in the world today. He has traveled extensively to 40 U.S. states, as well as the countries of Ethiopia, Mexico, Russia, Uganda and the Ukraine.

In his travels, David witnessed thousands of people make professions of faith in Jesus Christ. He has recruited over 4,000 people for evangelistic outreach and helped train hundreds in Biblical evangelism. Many of them are now leading others to Christ.

Early in his Christian walk, David experienced years of frustration in personal witnessing. Finally, he came to the understanding emphasized in this book - that it is God who opens the door for salvation. As this understanding took hold in David's life, things began to change, and people came to Christ.

God has called David to equip the saints for the work of ministry (Ephesians 4:11-12). He has spoken to many different groups of people regarding these personal evangelism principles. David Morel is the founder of *Biblical Evangelism Ministries, Inc.*

Biblical Evangelism Ministries, Inc. is a non-profit ministry, with the singular focus of training Christians in the area of Biblical evangelism.

For personal evangelism training, to obtain more copies of this book, or for additional evangelism resources contact David A. Morel at the following:

Biblical Evangelism Ministries, Inc.
625 Shute Lane
Old Hickory, TN 37138
800-800-2519
david@davidmorel.net
www.davidmorel.net

Mr. "W", the subject of this narrative, died in New York, about the year 1883, at the age of seventy-four. He was an avowed infidel (atheist). He was a good neighbor in some respects, yet he was very wicked and scoffed at Christianity. About seven years previous to his death, he passed through a revival. The Spirit strove with him, but he resisted to the last.

One Sabbath after this, Mr. "N" who relates this sketch, was on his way to church and passed Mr. W's house, who was standing by the gate. He said, "Come with me to church." The infidel, holding out his hand, replied, "Show me a hair on the palm of my hand and I will show you a Christian."

During his last sickness, Mr. "N" called on him often. He sat up with him several nights and was with him when he died. The infidel was conscious of his near approaching end and of the terrors of his lost condition. He said once to Mr. "N", who, as a local worker, held meetings in schoolhouses around, "Warn the world not to live as I have lived, and escape my woe." At another time when visited by a doctor, he was groaning and appeared to be in great agony. The doctor said, "Why do you groan, your disease is not painful?" "O, doctor," said he, "it is not the body but the soul that troubles me."

On the evening of his death, Mr. "N" came at ten o'clock. As he entered the room, he felt that it was filled with an awful presence - as if he were near the region of the damned. The dying man cried out, "O God, deliver me from that awful pit!" It was not a penitential prayer, but the wail of a lost soul. About fifteen minutes before his death, which was at twelve, he exclaimed, "I am in the flames - pull me out, pull me out!" He kept repeating this until the breath left his body. As the bodily strength failed, his words became more faint. At last Mr. "N" put his ear down close to catch his departing whispers, and the last words he could hear were, "Pull me out, pull me out!"

"It was an awful scene," said he. "It made an impression on me that I can never forget. I never want to witness such a scene again." I was talking with my friend years after, and he said those words, "I am in the flames - pull me out, pull me out!" were still ringing in his ears. *Written by the Reverend C.A. Balch, Cloverville, N.Y. - "The Dying Testimonies of Saved and Unsaved." - Page 100 - S.B. Shaw Publisher, Chicago, IL - 1898*

> *"So it will be at the end of the age. The angels will come forth, separate the wicked from among the just, and cast them into the furnace of fire. There will be wailing and gnashing of teeth."*   *Matthew 13:49-50*

It is clear from the Word of God that those who have never trusted Jesus Christ as their personal Savior will spend eternity in the endless lake of fire (Revelation 20:10). As we consider our family, friends, coworkers and acquaintances, we realize that many people we know may end up there someday. This is a daunting thought for those of us who are saved and will spend eternity with God. It is one reality that many of us have a deep desire to change. Yet, sharing Christ is often very uncomfortable for us, as well as for those with whom we share.

It is the aim of this book to explain why we are so uncomfortable and to share God's Biblical method for personal evangelism. When we follow the Biblical role model, we will find witnessing more comfortable and begin to encounter hungry hearts who want to know more about Christ.

We can never study enough, or be prepared enough, in witnessing for Christ. But, we do not have to wait until we are prepared to win people to Christ. We can start now. It is my opinion that Christians have made the soul-winning process far more difficult than God ever intended. In the beginning, God will bring people your way who need to hear the knowledge that you have. As you become more studied, God will bring more challenging people into your life. But the key is, don't wait! Lean on God and start now.

I trust this book will make your personal witnessing easier and more enjoyable than you have ever imagined. "The fruit of the righteous is a tree of life, And he who wins souls is wise" (Proverbs 11:30).

CHAPTER 1

THE MYSTERY OF THE GOSPEL

Have you ever wondered why people reject the gospel of Jesus Christ? After all, we will spend maybe 60, 80 or 100 years on this earth. Then, we will spend eternity either in the awesome presence of Almighty God or in the endless lake of fire (Revelation 20:10). Think about it! The gospel is the only thing that will keep people from burning in hell forever. It should be the one thing that the heart of man would desire above all else. So, why do people reject the gospel of Jesus Christ? Very simply, because the gospel is a mystery:

> *the mystery which has been hidden from ages and from generations, but now has been revealed to His saints. To them God willed to make known what are the riches of the glory of this mystery among the Gentiles: which is Christ in you, the hope of glory.*
> *Colossians 1:26-27*

The gospel has been hidden for ages and generations. It is a mystery to unbelievers. The apostle Paul confirms this in the following Scripture passage:

> *praying always with all prayer and supplication in the Spirit, . . . that utterance may be given to me, that I may open my mouth boldly to make known the mystery of the gospel.*
> *Ephesians 6:18-19*

Paul understood that the gospel is a mystery. The American Heritage Dictionary gives one definition of "mystery" as follows: *A religious truth that is incomprehensible to reason and knowable only through divine revelation.*[1]

The gospel is a mystery

This should help us understand our own experience in personal evangelism. Many people reject our claims and offer of eternal salvation through Jesus Christ simply because it is incomprehensible to them. Unbelievers do not come to Christ through mere reason. And thus, the vast majority of Christians are unsuccessful in soul-winning. Conservative estimates state that between 95% and 97% of all Christians have never led anyone to Christ.

The Bible also describes the gospel as being hidden from unbelievers like a veil over their eyes:

> *But even if our gospel is veiled, it is veiled to those who are perishing, whose minds the god of this age has blinded, who do not believe, lest the light of the gospel of the glory of Christ, who is the image of God, should shine on them.* *2 Corinthians 4:3-4*

This passage states that the god of this world has blinded their minds so they cannot understand. Therefore, sharing the gospel with an unbeliever would be like handing a book to a blind man and asking him to read it. He obviously cannot read the book.

The gospel is hidden like a veil over their eyes

3

The Bible puts the same concept still another way when it states that the message of the cross is foolishness to unbelievers:

> For the message of the cross is foolishness to those who are perishing, but to us who are being saved it is the power of God. For it is written: "I will destroy the wisdom of the wise, And bring to nothing the understanding of the prudent." Where is the wise? Where is the scribe? Where is the disputer of this age? Has not God made foolish the wisdom of this world? For since, in the wisdom of God, the world through wisdom did not know God, it pleased God through the foolishness of the message preached to save those who believe.
>
> 1 Corinthians 1:18-21

At first glance, the gospel doesn't make any sense to the unbeliever. He might say, "What do you mean? You're telling me that the Son of God died on a cross for my sins? And if I put my trust in Him, then I will have everlasting life?" They simply do not understand. The gospel is foolishness to them.

These passages clearly state that the gospel of Jesus Christ is a mystery to unbelievers. It simply doesn't make any sense to them. The devil has blinded their minds and therefore, the preaching of the cross is foolishness to those who are perishing. So, the task that lies before us (preaching the gospel) would seem to be a formidable one.

The gospel is foolishness to unbelievers

At this point, we may be tempted to throw in the towel before we even begin. After all, the Word of God is true; it cannot be broken (John 10:35). Yet, that same Word of God does not leave us an option. We have a mandate from our Savior to win the lost at any cost. We are called to make disciples of all nations:

> *"Go therefore and make disciples of all the nations, baptizing them in the name of the Father and of the Son and of the Holy Spirit, teaching them to observe all things that I have commanded you; and lo, I am with you always, even to the end of the age." Amen.*
> *Matthew 28:19-20*

And He said to them, "Go into all the world and preach the gospel to every creature."

Mark 16:15

So how do you and I break through this mystery? How do we open the eyes of the unbeliever? What will make the foolish gospel message become "the power of God to salvation for everyone who believes" (Romans 1:16)? This book will attempt to answer these questions and make you a fruitful witness for the Lord Jesus Christ. Take heart, "for with God all things are possible" (Mark 10:27).

(1) The American Heritage® Dictionary of the English Language, Fourth Edition - Copyright © 2000 by Houghton Mifflin Company.

CHAPTER 2

UNVEILING THE MYSTERY OF THE GOSPEL

The gospel is a mystery, as we have seen. It is foolishness to those who are perishing because the god of this world has blinded their mind. Nonetheless, the gospel can be unveiled. Take careful note of the following passage:

> He said to them, "But who do you say that I am?" Simon Peter answered and said, "You are the Christ, the Son of the living God." Jesus answered and said to him, "Blessed are you, Simon Bar-Jonah, for flesh and blood has not revealed this to you, but My Father who is in heaven."   Matthew 16:15-17

Simon Peter recognized that Jesus was the Christ, the Son of the living God. But Peter did not come to that realization himself. God the Father revealed it to him. God unveiled the mystery. The following passage clearly states that very thing:

7

But we speak the wisdom of God in a mystery, the hidden wisdom which God ordained before the ages for our glory, which none of the rulers of this age knew; for had they known, they would not have crucified the Lord of glory. But as it is written: "Eye has not seen, nor ear heard, Nor have entered into the heart of man The things which God has prepared for those who love Him." <u>But God has revealed them to us through His Spirit.</u> For the Spirit searches all things, yes, the deep things of God.

1 Corinthians 2:7-10

The gospel cannot enter the heart of man unless God reveals it to him. God reveals things to us by His Holy Spirit. Don't miss this! <u>The secret to soul-winning is God revealing Himself, to the heart of man, by His Holy Spirit.</u> In order for any unbeliever to come to the saving knowledge of the Lord Jesus Christ, God must reveal it to him - or, open a door. Note what Jesus says:

The secret to soul-winning is "God revealing Himself, to the heart of man, by His Holy Spirit"

8

"No one can come to Me unless the Father who sent Me draws him; and I will raise him up at the last day. It is written in the prophets, 'And they shall all be taught by God.' Therefore everyone who has heard and learned from the Father comes to Me."   John 6:44-45

And He said, "Therefore I have said to you that no one can come to Me unless it has been granted to him by My Father."   John 6:65

So the mystery begins to unveil. Salvation is of God; "for without Me you can do nothing" (John 15:5). God can break through the mystery, open the eyes of unbelievers, and draw them to His Son, Jesus Christ, for salvation. It is God who (opens a door) gives the increase in the harvest of souls:

Salvation is of God

Who then is Paul, and who is Apollos, but ministers through whom you believed, as the Lord gave to each one? I planted, Apollos watered, but God gave the increase. So then neither he who plants is anything, nor he who waters, but God who gives the increase.

1 Corinthians 3:5-7

We must gain a firm grasp of this fact. No one will ever accept Jesus Christ as Savior unless God is involved. God must draw the heart of the unbeliever to the Lord Jesus Christ. We must build on a firm foundation. If we think that WE are doing the work, no one will ever come to Christ. God will not share His glory with any man. But, He wants to use us in this evangelism process. Humility lies at the heart of the true soul-winner, because he recognizes God's involvement in the process. God must "open a door."

Humility lies at the heart of the true soul-winner

Many years ago, I learned this the hard way. I had studied the plan of salvation that I would present. I memorized key Scriptures that would answer common questions unbelievers might ask. I had done my homework and I was prepared to win the lost to Christ, or so I thought.

10

One day, the opportunity presented itself. My wife and I were at an outdoor party, relaxing and playing a game with another couple. Suddenly, the man made a derogatory remark toward my wife and I. It was an obvious attack on the fact that we were Christians. I thought, 'Well, you asked for it.'

You see, this was the day I had been preparing for. So I pulled out my sword and went straight for his jugular vein. About 15 minutes later, just like a little puppy licking his wounds from battle, there I was, totally defeated. The man continued to make a mockery of us. I was devastated by the fact that I was losing this battle of words.

I thought, 'God, how can this be? I am a student of your Word, and this man has never even cracked open a Bible. Why is this happening to me?' And God, in His infinite mercy spoke to my heart (no audible words, yet clear as a bell). I must tell you, it was as though He had stopped the whole world and had a personal conversation with only me. He said, "My son, who is doing the talking here, you or Me?"

I said, "Me." He said very simply, "Will you let Me do it?" <u>I began to pray</u>, "Yes God, but you're going to have to do something. I am at a total loss for words. You need to move on his heart. You need to give me the words to say."

Well, at that instant, God started the world moving again. I don't remember the next thing I said, but I will never forget the look on that man's face. His countenance changed and he said, "You know, I never really thought about it that way before." God had moved on his heart and turned the tide of the entire conversation. At that moment, I was overwhelmed. God taught me one of the most important lessons I have ever learned about witnessing - Humility! ". . . for without Me you can do nothing" (John 15:5).

We must have God's help in order to become effective in our personal witness. But, if God must reveal Himself to the unbeliever, what then is our involvement in this process? There are three primary elements to personal evangelism examined in the remainder of this book. These elements will build upon this firm foundation of "humility," or recognizing that God must open a door. They are as follows:

1) Prayer - Breaking Through the Mystery
2) The Bible - Revealing the Mystery
3) Faith - Stepping Out of the Comfort Zone

Hopefully, you are becoming excited about embarking on one of the most joy-filled aspects of the Christian life; soul-winning. I have participated in hundreds of witnessing opportunities with unbelievers. Each one was unique. Nonetheless, there were two elements common to all of them. First, was the noticeable presence of the Holy Spirit of God. Second, there was unspeakable joy.

We will now build on this firm foundation of knowing that, "God gave the increase" (1 Corinthians 3:6).

For no other foundation can anyone lay than that which is laid, which is Jesus Christ.
1 Corinthians 3:11

CHAPTER 3

PRAYER - BREAKING THROUGH THE MYSTERY

W e have seen that the gospel of Christ is a mystery to unbelievers and that we need God's help to unveil this mystery. The next element lies in our prayer life. I would like to address four aspects of prayer that are involved in evangelism. First, we must ask God to develop a burden in our hearts for the lost. Second, and I believe most importantly, we must ask God to unveil the mystery of the gospel to the unbeliever's heart, or to open a door. Third, we must ask God to fill our mouth with His words in proclaiming the gospel of Christ. Fourth, we must pray that God would grant us wisdom to answer all of the unbeliever's questions and objections.

DEVELOPING A BURDEN FOR THE LOST

The first aspect of prayer in evangelism is to pray that we become compassionate for the lost. We need to develop a burden for the lost. We need to recognize that they are hanging over those eternal flames, by a thread that could snap before their next breath. We must weep for the lost like the Psalmist who said, "Those who sow in tears Shall reap in joy. He who continually goes forth weeping, Bearing seed for sowing, Shall doubtless come again with rejoicing, Bringing his sheaves with him" (Psalm 126:5-6).

So how do we develop a burden for the lost? We need to ask God daily to burden our hearts for the lost. Prayer is the key!

We need to ask God daily to burden our hearts for the lost

One Saturday, my wife, two daughters and I were eating at a restaurant. It was the day before Easter. We noticed an intimidating young man at a table near us. He wore a shirt that said, "Bad Religion," and an expensive leather jacket. On the back of the jacket were inscribed the words, "Jesus Died for His Own Sins, Not Mine!"

When I noticed this, I wanted to "Punch his lights out!" But, God spoke to my heart saying, "What makes you any better than this young man?" I immediately came under conviction and began to pray, "God, I know you died for this young man too, but look at his jacket!" At that moment, I had no compassion for this lost man. I had finished eating, but my family had not, so I just closed my eyes and kept on praying. Then, something wonderful happened to me. When I opened my eyes and looked at him, I realized he was hanging over those flames by a thread. God changed my heart.

The young man and his girl friend got up to leave. I stopped him and said, "Excuse me sir, could I see the back of your jacket?" He spun around wild-eyed and proudly displayed the back of his jacket. I asked, "Do you really believe that?" He retorted, "Yeah, happy Easter," and he stormed out of the restaurant. Moved with compassion, I asked my wife and daughters to pray and I followed him out of the door. I approached him in the parking lot and caught him by surprise. He began to warm up as we talked about Jesus Christ. We talked for about 20 minutes. I would like to say that he surrendered his life to Christ that day, but he had a long way to go. Yet, for the first time in his life, that young man caught a glimpse of the fact that Jesus loved him and was not his enemy, but his friend.

It is not in our (sinful) nature to be compassionate for the lost. We have to ask God to burden our hearts for the lost. So, the first aspect of prayer is asking God to fill our hearts with compassion.

Breaking Through the Mystery

The second aspect of prayer in evangelism is asking God to unveil the mystery of the gospel. The following Scripture is perhaps the most important prayer one could ever pray in order to become a true soul-winner. It is found in the book of Colossians. Before examining this passage, stop and pray. Ask God for revelation on the truth that lies within.

> *Continue earnestly in prayer, being vigilant in it with thanksgiving; meanwhile praying also for us, that God would open to us a door for the word, to speak the mystery of Christ, for which I am also in chains, that I may make it manifest, as I ought to speak. Walk in wisdom toward those who are outside, redeeming the time. Let your speech always be with grace, seasoned with salt, that you may know how you ought to answer each one.* Colossians 4:2-6

You will recall from the first chapter that the gospel is a mystery to those who are perishing. In the second chapter we found that God must unveil that mystery. Now read the Colossians 4 prayer again; "praying . . . that God would open to us a door for the word, to speak the mystery of Christ." Do you see it? Do you see the importance of prayer in evangelism? The Colossians 4 prayer goes straight to the heart of the problem. It asks God to **BREAK THROUGH THE MYSTERY** of the gospel, to "open to us a door for the word, to speak the mystery of Christ."

This brings us to another very important point. I like to call it, Paul's open doors. Several times in the New Testament, the Apostle Paul stated that God had opened a door for him to share the gospel of Christ. We read that God, "had opened the door of faith to the Gentiles" (Acts 14:27). Paul said, "But I will tarry in Ephesus until Pentecost. For a great and effective door has opened to me" (1 Corinthians 16:8-9). Finally, he said, "Furthermore, when I came to Troas to preach Christ's gospel, and a door was opened to me by the Lord" (2 Corinthians 2:12). If we trace these open doors carefully, we will find that, in each case, people came to know Jesus Christ as their personal Savior. So why did Paul have so many open doors? I believe we can trace these open doors directly to Paul's prayer life as exemplified in Colossians 4:3, "open to us a door for the word." Therefore, we find that prayer is the *Secret to an Open Door.*

Prayer is the "Secret to an Open Door"

Don't miss this! We are now embarking on the threshold of becoming true soul-winners. Remember that salvation is of God. He must be involved. We must pray specifically for God to "open to us a door for the word, to speak the mystery of Christ." If we ask, He will open a door!

> *"I know your works. See, I have set before you an open door, and no one can shut it."*
>
> *Revelation 3:8*

The Colossians 4 prayer goes right to the very heart of God. God is "not willing that any should perish but that all should come to repentance" (2 Peter 3:9).

This verse plainly tells us that it is the will of God that none should perish. Here it is again:

For this is good and acceptable in the sight of God our Savior, who desires all men to be saved and to come to the knowledge of the truth. 1 Timothy 2:3-4

The reason the Colossians 4 prayer is so powerful is that you are praying a Scriptural prayer. Therefore, it is a prayer in the will of God. When we pray according to His will, He will respond:

Now this is the confidence that we have in Him, that if we ask anything according to His will, He hears us. And if we know that He hears us, whatever we ask, we know that we have the petitions that we have asked of Him.
1 John 5:14-15

I boarded a plane a few years ago. As I was walking down the aisle toward my seat, I prayed the Colossians 4 prayer. Within minutes, a young man in military uniform came and sat in the seat next to me. I asked him about his service in the military.

The plane took off and we had a very pleasant conversation. He was 24 years old and *(Watch This!)* the thought just entered my mind, 'He sure has his

head screwed on right for a 24-year old.' So, I just looked at him and said, "You sure have your head screwed on right for a 24-year old." He looked at me puzzled and said, "No, you don't know me very well," and he began to pour out his heart.

The Colossians 4 prayer is a prayer that is in God's will

The young man was besieged with personal problems and was hurting deeply. I pulled out a New Testament and showed him that God's Word offers help in dealing with life's situations. He was very grateful and said, "That's just what I need." After a little more discussion, I shared the plan of salvation with him. He then turned and looked at me with eternity in his eyes and said, "God put you next to me, didn't He?" I said, "Let me tell you what I prayed as I got on the plane," and I quoted the Colossians 4 prayer. Tears began streaming down his face.

How could you or I ever orchestrate something like this? This is the handiwork of a sovereign God in answer to specific prayer. This is the *Secret to an Open Door*. Notice also that the conversation was normal. There were no crafty words, or carefully structured answers, just conversation guided by the hand of God. In case you think this is just a coincidence, I will share another story later in the chapter that reaffirms the power of specific prayer in personal witnessing.

GOD GIVES US THE WORDS

The third aspect of prayer in evangelism is asking God to put His words in our mouth, so that we might boldly proclaim the gospel of Christ. You will note, that is exactly what God did in the previous story. Let's look at another portion of the Colossians 4 prayer; "That I may make it manifest, as I ought to speak" (Colossians 4:4). By praying this way, we ask God to help us present the gospel so the unbeliever will hear, understand, and receive the Lord Jesus Christ as Savior. Prayer is vital because this presentation will be different each time we witness. Only God knows what they will hear and receive from us. He must be involved in the process and give us the words to speak. Paul understood the importance of this aspect of prayer and confirms it in the book of Ephesians:

> *praying always with all prayer and supplication in the Spirit, being watchful to this end with all perseverance and supplication for all the saints--and for me, that utterance may be given to me, that I may open my mouth boldly to make known the mystery of the gospel, for which I am an ambassador in chains; that in it I may speak boldly, as I ought to speak.*
>
> *Ephesians 6:18-20*

This follows one of the most famous Scripture passages of all time. In Ephesians 6:10-20, we are admonished to put on the whole armor of God. Paul then concludes by saying, "praying always . . . that utterance may be given to me, that I may open my mouth boldly to make known the mystery of the gospel . . . that in it I may speak boldly, as I ought to speak." We are fighting a spiritual battle for the

24

eternal souls of unbelievers. Therefore, <u>we need to suit up in the full armor of God</u> and then, "praying always . . . that I may <u>open my mouth boldly</u>."

It is important to notice one more element in the previous passage. Paul was praying specifically for boldness when sharing the gospel of Christ. Certainly, most of us <u>need more courage</u> when it

Pray that you may speak the gospel boldly

comes to witnessing to the lost. In the following passage we see that God very clearly answered the disciples' prayer for boldness in speaking forth the word of God:

> *Now, Lord, look on their threats, and grant to Your servants that with all boldness they may speak Your word . . . And when they had <u>prayed</u>, the place where they were assembled together was shaken; and they were all filled with the Holy Spirit, and they spoke the word of God with boldness.*
>
> *Acts 4:29, 31*

Answering the Unbeliever's Questions

The fourth aspect of prayer in evangelism is knowing how to answer all of the unbeliever's questions, doubts or objections. It is also found in the Colossians 4 prayer; "Let your speech always be with grace, seasoned with salt, that you may know how you ought to answer each one" (Colossians 4:6). Again, the emphasis is upon prayer. Paul said to pray, "that you may know how you ought to answer each one." God will give us specific words in answer to specific prayer. God will help us to "be ready to give a defense to everyone who asks you a reason for the hope that is in you, with meekness and fear" (1 Peter 3:15).

You might be thinking, 'This is a great theological discussion, but what about me? I just want to be an effective witness for Christ. How does all of this apply to me?' I believe this will actually become very practical in your life. If you pray these prayers, (Colossians 4:2-6 and Ephesians 6:18-20) you will find yourself becoming an effective witness. You will find that your normal, daily conversations with unbelievers will naturally turn to the subject of Jesus

Christ and Him crucified. The answers to their questions (supernaturally given by God) will become your normal thoughts as you speak with them. Personal witnessing God's way (fervent prayer) is a very natural thing. Of course, you will still be required to step out in faith and open your mouth boldly to speak the gospel of Christ.

THE POWER OF SPECIFIC PRAYER

I was preparing a message on personal witnessing to give to a group of people. As I was putting the outline together, I realized that I must share about the power of specific prayer, or the *Secret to an Open Door.* So often I had seen God move powerfully in response to the Colossians 4 prayer. Again, God spoke to my heart, "How long has it been since you have prayed that prayer?" Due to the busyness of recent days, I realized it had been several months since I had prayed that specific prayer. Well, I was under conviction. So that night and the next morning, I got serious with God and spent some time in intercession with the focus in Colossians of, "open to us a door for the word, to speak the mystery of Christ" (Colossians 4:3).

I landed at Chicago Midway airport that day and had to make a connecting flight. I stood in line at the ticket counter and there were about thirty people in front of me. Then I noticed the young lady behind me was reading a "Beanie Baby" magazine. My daughter loved beanie babies and was looking for a book that had prices of all of the beanie babies. I asked her if it had the prices and she said, "Yes, you can get them over there at the newsstand." That started a conversation and we talked about various things. By the time we reached the ticket counter, as God would have it, the conversation had gone to the deeper things in life.

As I handed my tickets to the person behind the counter, this young lady said to me, "My baby was born dead (still born) two weeks ago." I was shocked and totally at a loss for words. I pulled out a New Testament and gave it to her. I said, "I don't know what to say, but I know One who does," and I told her the answers she sought were in here. I sat down while she was getting her tickets and I began to pray. A few minutes later, she came over to me and asked if she could sit next to me. She began to pour out her heart and then she asked, "Is God punishing me because of my sins?" God was at work in her heart! I was able to show her Scriptures that gave her some comfort. Then, I shared the gospel message with her.

I flew on to my next destination. While walking through the airport, I noticed a man who was on the flight with me and I said, "Weren't you on that flight from Chicago?" He said, "Yes, I was." We began to talk as we walked along. I asked him if he would like a New Testament. He said, "Yes." As we talked he slowly began to confess to me that he had committed adultery. Imagine my shock. I had met this man less than five minutes before. He said, "Have you got a minute?" I said, "Of course." We spent some time talking and he shared what had happened. Then he asked, "Can God forgive me?" We read a passage about forgiveness and then I shared God's plan of salvation with him.

The point of this story is obvious. These opportunities were a direct result of praying the Colossians 4 prayer and expectant faith. God answers specific prayers, especially those that are according to His will. As we have seen, praying for the lost is always a prayer in God's will. Also, please note that these conversations were very natural and normal. I didn't use any witnessing techniques or fancy words. God simply turned the conversation toward spiritual matters. If we pray these prayers (Colossians 4:2-6 & Ephesians 6:18-20) and get serious with God about this matter of soul-winning, He will get serious with us. Why don't you give it a try? Souls are hanging over those eternal flames, by a thread!

Dear Lord, please "open to us a door for the word, to speak the mystery of Christ" (Colossians 4:3).

CHAPTER 4

THE BIBLE - REVEALING THE MYSTERY

Prayer moves the hand of God, who then begins to unveil the mystery of the gospel. Another element crucial to revealing the mystery of the gospel is the Word of God. In chapter 1, we saw that the devil has blinded the eyes of the unbeliever. With that in mind, consider the following verse:

The statutes of the LORD are right, rejoicing the heart; The commandment of the LORD is pure, enlightening the eyes   *Psalm 19:8*

Here we see that God's Word enlightens, or opens, the eyes of the unbeliever, so they are no longer blind. We also saw in Chapter 1 that the gospel is foolishness to those who are perishing. Again, consider the following:

The entrance of Your words gives light; It gives understanding to the simple.   *Psalm 119:130*

Here we see that God's Word gives understanding so that the foolish gospel may be understood.

Whether the unbeliever hears the spoken Word or whether he simply reads it, the Bible begins to reveal the mystery of the gospel. The Word of God is living and powerful. When we are confronted with God's Holy Word, it brings to light the truth in our thoughts and intentions. God's Word bares the very heart of man. This is all confirmed in the following passage:

For the word of God is living and powerful, and sharper than any two-edged sword, piercing even to the division of soul and spirit, and of joints and marrow, and is a discerner of the thoughts and intents of the heart. Hebrews 4:12

Since the Word of God is such a crucial element in revealing the mystery of the gospel, how important is it that you and I spend time in God's Word? We need a daily routine to soak up God's Holy Word. We must study the Bible carefully and prayerfully:

Be diligent to present yourself approved to God, a worker who does not need to be ashamed, rightly dividing the word of truth.

2 Timothy 2:15

God is looking for soldiers in this battle for the eternal souls of unbelievers; soldiers who have studied and are "ready to give a defense to everyone who asks you a reason for the hope that is in you, with meekness and fear" (1 Peter 3:15).

THE WORD IS A WEAPON

An offensive weapon in this battle for souls is "the sword of the Spirit, which is the word of God" (Ephesians 6:17). In Matthew 4:1-10, we read that Jesus was led by the Spirit into the wilderness to be tempted by the devil. It would be wise for us to take careful note of the ensuing battle:

Then Jesus was led up by the Spirit into the wilderness to be tempted by the devil. And when He had fasted forty days and forty nights, afterward He was hungry. Now when the tempter came to Him, he said, "If You are the Son of God, command that these stones become bread." But He answered and said, "It is written, 'Man shall not live by bread alone, but by every word that proceeds from the mouth of God.'" Then the devil took Him up into the holy city, set Him on the pinnacle of the temple, and said to Him, "If You are the Son of God, throw Yourself down. For it is written: 'He shall give His angels charge over you,' and, 'In their hands they shall bear you up, Lest you dash your foot against a stone.'" Jesus said to him, "It is written again, 'You shall not tempt the LORD your God.'" Again, the devil took Him up on an exceedingly high mountain, and showed Him all the kingdoms of the world and their glory. And he said to Him, "All these things I will give You if You will fall down and worship me." Then Jesus said to him, "Away with you, Satan! For it is written, 'You shall worship the LORD your God, and Him only you shall serve.'"   *Matthew 4:1-10*

Jesus fought the devil by quoting God's Word

In all three cases where Jesus was tempted by the devil, He said, "It is written." Then, He quoted Scripture. If Jesus fought the spiritual battle by quoting God's Holy Word, should we do any less? The Word of God quoted during personal witnessing has a profound impact upon the unbeliever. It does not return void. This brings us to a powerful portion of God's Word:

So shall My word be that goes forth from My mouth; It shall not return to Me void, But it shall accomplish what I please, And it shall prosper in the thing for which I sent it.

Isaiah 55:11

Now the very fact that God's Word does not return void, means that it doesn't always bring forth warm results. His Word is sharp as a two-edged sword and brings forth conviction of sin. This is a positive thing when witnessing, but the unbeliever's response to that conviction may not always be positive. When you share the gospel of Jesus

The Word of God does not return void

Christ, there is no way of knowing what the unbeliever's reaction will be. You are, in a nice way, telling them that they are a sinner in desperate need of a Savior. We must realize that we are not responsible for bringing forth warm results. We are responsible for bringing people to a realization of their need for a personal relationship with Jesus Christ. This is the very essence of personal witnessing.

Quoting God's Word is so powerful that the devil is going to try to sidetrack you. Sometimes unbelievers will say, "Stop quoting the Bible, I don't believe that book anyway." We may be tempted to try to win them by using our reasoning or concepts outside of the Bible. One well-known and respected pastor, when confronted in this way, said, "I just keep quoting the Bible anyway." The reason is found in the passages above. God's Word is alive, it is powerful, and it will not return void. Resist the temptation to find other ways, and continue (lovingly) sharing God's Word.

THE IMPORTANCE OF MEMORIZATION

Since quoting God's Word is such an important weapon in this battle for souls, it follows then, that it is very important to know and memorize God's Word. Many Christian bookstores carry Topical Memory Systems, which are designed to facilitate Scripture memorization. Some contain verses for presenting the gospel message and verses that provide answers to the unbeliever's questions. Memorizing Scripture will certainly make you a more effective witness.

You may be thinking, 'I just can't memorize anything.' However, I believe you can. Picture yourself driving down the road alone in your car. A song comes on the radio that you really enjoy, and you just start singing along. Guess what, you memorized something and you didn't even realize it. The fact is, anyone can memorize God's Word; it is simply a matter of repetition. Anything you say enough times, or listen to enough times, will be committed to memory.

One way to memorize a Bible verse is to read it over and over again onto a cassette tape. This repetition begins the memorization process. Then play the tape back and listen to it over and over. Next, repeat the verse along with the tape. Before you know it, the verse is memorized.

Another good way is to take the verse and break it down into short phrases. Say one phrase over and over again. When you have it down, go on to the next phrase. Apply a little discipline and before you know it, the verse is memorized. Finally, it is good to repeat Bible verses, weekly for a while, so that you do not forget them.

As a side note, you will gain much more benefit from Scripture memorization than simply being a better witness for Christ. This will greatly improve your spiritual life as well. Note the following passages from God's Word:

> *Therefore you shall lay up these words of mine in your heart and in your soul, and bind them as a sign on your hand, and they shall be as frontlets between your eyes.*
>
> *Deuteronomy 11:18*

> *"This Book of the Law shall not depart from your mouth, but you shall meditate in it day and night, that you may observe to do according to all that is written in it. For then you will make your way prosperous, and then you will have good success."*   *Joshua 1:8*

But his delight is in the law of the LORD, And in His law he meditates day and night. He shall be like a tree Planted by the rivers of water, That brings forth its fruit in its season, Whose leaf also shall not wither; And whatever he does shall prosper.   *Psalm 1:2-3*

Two of these passages refer to meditating day and night on God's Word. The easiest (perhaps, only) way we can do this is by committing Scripture to memory.

When we meditate day and night on God's Word, we will prosper, have good success, and be like a tree planted near water, bearing fruit and not withering. Also, we are less likely to sin if we hide God's Word in our hearts. Psalm

Meditate day and night on God's Word

119:11 says, "Your word I have hidden in my heart, That I might not sin against You!"

There are numerous reasons to memorize Scripture, not the least of which is that Scripture itself tells us to do so. As a Christian, your personal relationship with

The Holy Spirit will bring God's Word to memory

Jesus Christ will certainly be enhanced. As previously stated personal witnessing will be easier because the Holy Spirit will bring these verses to memory at the proper time. Jesus said,

"But the Helper, the Holy Spirit, whom the Father will send in My name, He will teach you all things, and bring to your remembrance all things that I said to you." John 14:26

THE POWER OF THE WORD TO SAVE

Finally, and most importantly, is the power of God's Word to save the lost soul. The following verses stress the importance of God's Word in bringing people to a saving knowledge of the Lord Jesus Christ:

The law of the LORD is perfect, converting the soul. Psalm 19:7

having been born again, not of corruptible seed but incorruptible, through the word of God which lives and abides forever. 1 Peter 1:23

Also, Scripture plainly tells us that we are saved by grace through faith; and faith comes by hearing the Word of God:

For "whoever calls on the name of the LORD shall be saved." How then shall they call on Him in whom they have not believed? And how shall they believe in Him of whom they have not heard? And how shall they hear without a preacher? And how shall they preach unless they are sent? As it is written: "How beautiful are the feet of those who preach the gospel of peace, Who bring glad tidings of good things!" But they have not all obeyed the gospel. For Isaiah says, "Lord, who has believed our report?" So then faith comes by hearing, and hearing by the word of God. Romans 10:13-17

A major protestant denomination conducted a survey[1] of 1,350 people who were baptized between October 1, 1992 and September 30, 1993. All were age 18 or older. One question on the survey included 11 potential items that influenced the person's decision to receive Jesus Christ as Savior. The respondents could list more than one item as making a major contribution to their conversion. Attending church worship services was the number one influence, listed by 76.9% of those surveyed. The second most commonly named influence, "reading the Bible on your own," was listed by 57.5% of the respondents. This can only underscore the power of God's Holy Word to reveal the mystery of the gospel and bring people to Christ.

Faith comes by hearing the Word of God

A TESTIMONY

The following story points out the importance of sharing God's Word when He opens a door of opportunity. It was God's Word, and the Holy Spirit, that caused this young man to come to Christ. For the Bible is, "the implanted word, which is able to save your souls" (James 1:21).

A carpenter was driving home after a long, but satisfying, day at work. He was contemplating the fine work he had accomplished on the home that he was building. Suddenly, he passed by a hitchhiker.

God spoke to his heart, "What have you done for Me lately?" He realized that God was telling him to pick up the young man, so he stopped. The young man got into his car and they drove off down the road.

The carpenter began a conversation and the hitch-hiker's first words were, "I sure am glad to be out of prison." The carpenter wondered if he had made a mistake. He looked for his Bible, which he usually kept on the dash of his truck, but it wasn't there. The young man asked, "What are you looking for?" He replied, "My Bible." The young man reached in his duffel bag, pulled out a New Testament, and said, "You mean like this?" "Yes," replied the carpenter. "I got it in prison," he said.

The young man admitted that he wasn't saved, so the carpenter asked him to read John 3:16. He guided him to the location of the passage and the young man read the verse out loud. "What does that mean to you?" asked the carpenter. "I don't get it," he replied. "Read it again," said the carpenter. So, the young man read the verse out loud again. "Now, do you understand it?" he asked. The puzzled young man said, "No."

"Read it again," said the carpenter. The young man read John 3:16 aloud for a third time and something wonderful happened. With tears streaming down his face, the young man said, "Now I understand. Jesus died for me, too!" They stopped the truck and the young man bowed his head and prayed to receive Jesus Christ as his personal Savior.

In summary, we have discussed several truths about God's Holy Word. It reveals the mystery of the gospel to unbelievers. Combined with the Holy Spirit, God's Word brings sin to light, causes conviction over that sin, and points the unbeliever to a need for a Savior. Also, God's Word is an offensive weapon in this battle for the souls of unbelievers. Finally, saving faith comes by hearing the Word of God. Thus, it is crucial for us to study and be equipped with God's Word, so the Holy Spirit can bring it to our remembrance at the proper time. Then, we shall become effective soul-winners.

If you are still unsure of the importance of God's Word in evangelism, then review the following Scriptures prayerfully:

The law of the LORD is perfect, converting the soul. Psalm 19:7

having been born again, not of corruptible seed but incorruptible, through the word of God which lives and abides forever. 1 Peter 1:23

"Is not My word like a fire?" says the LORD, "And like a hammer that breaks the rock in pieces?" Jeremiah 23:29

Therefore lay aside all filthiness and overflow of wickedness, and receive with meekness the implanted word, which is able to save your souls. James 1:21

So shall My word be that goes forth from My mouth; It shall not return to Me void, But it shall accomplish what I please, And it shall prosper in the thing for which I sent it.
                                                    Isaiah 55:11

(1) The Baptist Standard, page 18, May 3, 1995.

CHAPTER 5

FAITH - STEPPING OUT OF THE COMFORT ZONE

We have seen that prayer and God's Word are two important weapons in this battle for the soul of the unbeliever. But, up to this point, all is in vain unless we step out in faith. Let's face it. It's often uncomfortable to share our faith with an unbeliever. But, here is an empowering revelation for you. God does not want us in our comfort zone! That is what "faith" is all about:

For we walk by faith, not by sight.
2 Corinthians 5:7

One day I read this passage and it became abundantly clear to me, that much of my life I had walked by sight and not by faith. As I pondered this, I realized that God had often called me out of my comfort zone and I was unwilling to go. I didn't want to witness to my neighbor, even though I could sense God telling me I should. I didn't want to stop and help that stranded motorist. Yet, for miles after, that gnawing sense stayed with me. Yes, God wanted to use me to share the gospel, but I was afraid to walk by faith. I wasn't sure what to say, and I didn't trust God to give me the words. I wanted to walk by sight.

Be willing to get out of your comfort zone

The Apostle Peter got out of his comfort zone when he stepped out of the boat. Then, he walked on water. Now that's faith! Everyone wants to walk on water, but no one wants to get out of the boat. That's outside of the comfort zone.

Moses said, "No," to God four times before he finally answered the call to deliver the Israelites out of Egypt. Moses wanted to stay in his comfort zone. Let's look at one of those four excuses:

Then Moses said to the LORD, "O my Lord, I am not eloquent, neither before nor since You have spoken to Your servant; but I am slow of

speech and slow of tongue." So the LORD said
to him, "Who has made man's mouth? Or who
makes the mute, the deaf, the seeing, or the
blind? Have not I, the LORD? Now therefore,
go, and I will be with your mouth and teach you
what you shall say."   *Exodus 4:10-12*

Moses wasn't sure what to say and he didn't trust God
to give him the words. Isn't it interesting what God
said to him? "Now therefore, go, and I will be with
your mouth and teach you what you shall say." God
promised Moses that He would give him the very
words that he should speak. But, Moses didn't believe
Him. In order to receive the promise, we have to step
out in faith, believing the promise - "the word which
they heard did not profit them, not being mixed with
faith in those who heard it" (Hebrews 4:2).

Let's look at another example in the Old Testament
character of Gideon:

Then the LORD turned to him and said, "Go in
this might of yours, and you shall save Israel

from the hand of the Midianites. Have I not sent you?" So he said to Him, "O my Lord, how can I save Israel? Indeed my clan is the weakest in Manasseh, and I am the least in my father's house." And the LORD said to him, "Surely I will be with you, and you shall defeat the Midianites as one man." Judges 6:14-16

Step out in faith

Gideon took a step of faith and defeated the Midianites, just as God had said. He went forth in faith. But faith based on what? On the promise of God, "Surely I will be with you." Now maybe you're saying, "Yeah, but he had a direct, clear and precise promise from God. If I had that same promise, I would be willing to get out of my comfort zone and take a step of faith." Dear saints, we have that exact same promise from God when it comes to personal witnessing. He will be with us.

"Go therefore and make disciples of all the nations, baptizing them in the name of the Father and of the Son and of the Holy Spirit,

teaching them to observe all things that I have commanded you; and lo, I am with you always, even to the end of the age." Amen.

Matthew 28:19-20

When it comes to personal witnessing, or making disciples, Jesus promised that He will be with us always. So, now we must simply be willing to get out of our comfort zone and take a step of faith. When we do, God will give us the words to share, just as He has promised.

As I began to learn that God would put His words in my mouth, some exciting things started to happen. One night I was working late, cramming for a work-related exam. The janitor was making his rounds and came by my office. We exchanged some pleasantries; he vacuumed my office and then was on his way.

God will put His words in your mouth

The thought *(Watch This!)* had crossed my mind, 'He is a really nice guy. I wonder if he is a Christian.'

I continued studying for the exam until after 9:00 p.m. and finally I couldn't keep my eyes open any longer. I grabbed my briefcase and headed for the elevator. As I did, the janitor walked by and said, "Calling it an evening?" I said, "Yes," and jumped on the elevator. Then, God spoke to my heart, "Go and witness to him."

Now, I was really out of my comfort zone. All I could think of was going home and going to bed. I was really fighting God. Besides, what would I say? Finally, realizing that this was not an excuse, I headed toward the direction I saw him last. I prayed, "Oh Lord, I'll go, but You will have to give me the words."

As I walked up to him, I caught him by surprise and startled him. He said, "Can I help you?" Still waiting on God, my mind was totally blank, except for my earlier thought. So, I said, "I was wondering, you seem to be a really nice guy. Are you a Christian?" The most amazing thing happened. He hung his head and said, "No, but my wife and I have been thinking about finding a church." Well, this began the most wonderful conversation and I was able to share the gospel with him.

God will give us the words. Often they are simply the very thoughts we are thinking, as seen above. Those thoughts come from the Holy Spirit of God. It will be as natural as carrying on a conversation, if we are praying and trusting God. We will become like Moses, when he finally answered the call to go. God was with him and gave him the words to say. But, we must be willing to get out of the comfort zone and take that step of faith.

It is well worth noting one more element in this story. Some people have since told me, "Don't ever ask someone if they are a Christian. Many unbelievers consider themselves to be a Christian, since they do not feel they are Hindu, Buddhist or Muslim." I agree that this is true. This question may force you to explain exactly who, or what, is a Christian. It can put the unbeliever in the awkward position of having to defend himself and bog down the conversation.

However, we must not be trapped in a mold. I have read and heard about many witnessing techniques, and most of them are good. But remember, they are simply techniques, while salvation is of God. Only God knows what needs to be shared with any one individual. That is why walking by faith, and trusting the Holy Spirit to bring to mind the right words, is so very important. Jesus said,

> *"But the Helper, the Holy Spirit, whom the Father will send in My name, He will teach you all things, and bring to your remembrance all things that I said to you."* John 14:26

Finally, it would be helpful to look at the great prophet of God, Jeremiah. He was used by God to proclaim a very difficult message of doom to the people of Israel. Jeremiah was even considered, by many people of his day, to be a traitor. But, he faithfully carried the message of God under circumstances far more difficult than you and I will likely face in our evangelistic efforts. Sometimes we look at these Old Testament characters as "bigger than life," or, as something supernaturally beyond you and I. But, according to James, they were ordinary people just like us, for "Elijah was a man with a nature like ours" (James 5:17). This should give us great hope. Consider Jeremiah's excuse in the following passage:

> *Then said I: "Ah, Lord GOD! Behold, I cannot speak, for I am a youth." But the LORD said to me: "Do not say, 'I am a youth,' For you shall go to all to whom I send you, And whatever I command you, you shall speak. Do not be afraid of their faces, For I am with you to deliver you," says the LORD. Then the LORD put forth His hand and touched my mouth, and the LORD said to me: "Behold, I have put My words in your mouth."* Jeremiah 1:6-9

Jeremiah was afraid to get out of his comfort zone. He didn't feel capable. But God said, "Behold, I have put My words in your mouth." After God had spoken, Jeremiah had just enough faith to believe that He would give him the words to say, and thus, the great success of his ministry.

The resounding question is, "Do we have enough faith to believe God?" If we stay committed to prayer, we can trust Him to "be with your mouth and teach you what you shall say" (Exodus 4:12). We can trust him to be "with you always, even to the end of the age" (Matthew 28:20). When we get out of our comfort zone, we too will experience God "put My words in your mouth" (Jeremiah 1:9). And finally, don't forget that the Holy Spirit will "bring to your remembrance all things that I said to you" (John 14:26).

Are we willing to get out of our comfort zone and "walk by faith, not by sight" (2 Corinthians 5:7)? If you are still not sure that God will put His words in your mouth, then may I suggest that you meditate carefully on the following Scripture passage:

"As for Me," says the LORD, "this is My covenant with them: My Spirit who is upon you, and My words which I have put in your mouth, shall not depart from your mouth, nor from the mouth of your descendants, nor from the mouth of your descendants' descendants," says the LORD, "from this time and forevermore."

Isaiah 59:21

CHAPTER 6

PERSONAL WITNESSING - THE PROCESS

If you decided to "cut to the chase" and started reading in this chapter, there is a good chance you will be disappointed. Perhaps you are looking for just the right technique that will make you a better soul-winner. The most effective "techniques" I have to offer are clearly laid out in the first five chapters of this book. They include prayer, Scripture study and memorization, and stepping out in faith. Finally, having done all of this, keep in mind that it is God who opens the door.

Now, you are ready to get out of your comfort zone and "walk by faith, not by sight" (2 Corinthians 5:7). Like Isaiah, you have "heard the voice of the Lord, saying, 'Whom shall I send, and who will go for Us?'" And you have responded, "Here am I! send me" (Isaiah 6:8). Perhaps you are excited about becoming a more effective witness for the Lord Jesus Christ. So, what's next?

Personal witnessing is generally a three-step process as follows:

1) The Open Door
2) Sharing the Gospel
3) Leading to a Decision

The Open Door

Here we come to the reason the first five chapters of this book are so important. As we have seen, you and I cannot open the door to witnessing opportunities. Remember, in the first chapter we saw that the gospel is "the mystery which has been hidden from ages and from generations" (Colossians 1:26); the gospel "is foolishness to those who are perishing" (1 Corinthians 1:18); and "it is veiled to those . . . whose minds the god of this age has blinded" (2 Corinthians 4:3-4).

In the second chapter, we saw that it is God who opens the door to soul-winning, for Jesus said, "No one can come to Me unless the Father who sent Me draws him" (John 6:44). Finally, in the third chapter we found that through prayer, God would "open to us a door for the word, to speak the mystery of Christ" (Colossians 4:3).

Here is where most witnessing techniques fail. Techniques rely on man, the depth of his knowledge and the extent of his abilities, to open the door to witnessing opportunities. But as Jesus just told us, opening the door is God's job. Biblical evangelism relies on God and fully expects Him to "open to us a door for the word, to speak the mystery of Christ" (Colossians 4:3).

It is important that we pray daily for these open doors. In so doing, we will lay the groundwork for God to open a door for us to share the gospel of Christ. These opportunities will simply begin to present themselves: at work, the grocery store, the gas station, on a plane, with neighbors, family, friends, acquaintances, etc. When the opportunity arises we must recognize it. More importantly, we must be willing to get out of our comfort zone and "walk by faith, not by sight" (2 Corinthians 5:7).

In most of the testimonies found in this book, you will notice that I gave a New Testament to the people with whom I was sharing. I carry them with me wherever I go; in my briefcase, in my car, or in my pocket. When an opportunity presents itself, I am quick to offer a copy of God's Word. I have found His Word to be the most incredible tool in personal witnessing. When people begin to read it, it often captivates them. In chapter four we saw the power of God's Word to reveal the mystery of the gospel and, of course, "faith comes by hearing, and hearing by the word of God" (Romans 10:17).

I suggest that you buy New Testaments in bulk. You can purchase them from most local Christian bookstores for less than $3.00 each. Isn't a soul worth $3.00? You should carry them with you wherever you go and ask God to open doors to give them to someone in need. You will be absolutely amazed at the number of doors God will open when you pray and are prepared to give them His Word.

God's Word is a powerful tool in witnessing

Most people will accept this gift if presented properly and it is very helpful as you share the gospel of the Lord Jesus Christ. There are as many ways to present a New Testament to someone as there are individuals presenting them. In time, you will develop methods of presentation with which you are comfortable. You might say, "I have a gift I would like to give you?" Or possibly, "Would you like a free copy of God's Word?"

Regardless of your method, be sure to point out some Scripture verses that are available to help them. In chapter seven there is a list of "Bible Verses for Different Needs." When most unbelievers are confronted with the Bible, they immediately feel condemnation. They have avoided the Bible all of their life because the devil has told them it would only condemn them. They need to see that God's Word

Unbelievers need to know the Bible was written to help them

was written to help them. The importance of this must never be underestimated as it will often cause them to want to read God's Word. Usually, at this point, you have made a friend. It is not uncommon to receive a warm, "Thank you," from the recipient.

Remember, we must continue to pray and ask God to give us the words to share. Salvation is of God; He must be involved. Pray that you may speak the mystery of Christ and that you may make it manifest, as you ought to speak (Colossians 4:3-4). The reason prayer is so important is the conversation can go in any one of a hundred different directions. God must guide our conversation and He will! We must learn to trust Him and expect Him to lead the conversation. After all, He has called us to "preach the gospel to every creature" (Mark 16:15); and promised us, "I am with you always" (Matthew 28:20).

SHARING THE GOSPEL

We must somehow make our way to God's plan of salvation. Again, there are many different things you could say to start the conversation. You might ask, "Do you know for sure that you would go to heaven if you died today?" You could ask, "Have you ever considered becoming a Christian?" Or, "Are you interested in spiritual things?" Don't be trapped in a mold. What works one time, may not work the next. You must pray and be sensitive to the leading of the Holy Spirit so God can do for you what he did for Jeremiah, "Behold, I have put My words in your mouth" (Jeremiah 1:9).

Perhaps you could share something similar to the following which is quite effective at gaining the unbeliever's attention:

> "When I was young, it seemed clear to me that Billy Graham was going to heaven when he died. It also seemed clear that Adolph Hitler was not. But, somewhere between the two, there was this dividing line. I always wondered where that dividing line was. How good is good enough to get to heaven? Have you ever wondered that? The Bible tells us exactly where that dividing line is!"

You likely have their attention and can now review the plan of salvation with them. Scripture tells us exactly where that dividing line is: "There is none righteous, no, not one" (Romans 3:10). It is very important for unbelievers to grasp this truth. As long as they believe that they can be "good enough" to get to heaven, they will not realize their need for a Savior. In most cases, the devil has reinforced this lie for many years. They must come face-to-face with the fact that they are sinners. Regardless of how good they are, they cannot get to heaven without receiving Jesus Christ as their Savior.

For by grace you have been saved through faith, and that not of yourselves; it is the gift of God, not of works, lest anyone should boast.
Ephesians 2:8-9

If time permits, when sharing the plan of salvation, do not be in a hurry. It is very important that you cover each step carefully. Read the Scriptures slowly, deliberately and, most importantly, prayerfully. It is even better if you can encourage the unbeliever to read the Scriptures out loud to you. And, of course, you are praying while they do. Each step of the way, ask them, "What does that verse say to you?" Or "What do you think God is trying to say?" In this way, they begin to tell you how they can be saved and,

likely, the Holy Spirit will be helping them out at this point. If they don't give the right answer, don't correct them. Simply have them look up another verse that applies to that part of God's plan and ask them again, "What does

Encourage them to read the Scriptures out loud

that verse say to you?" Be sure to pray without ceasing, asking God to "open to us a door for the word" (Colossians 4:3).

Remember, "the word of God is living and powerful, and sharper than any two-edged sword . . . and is a discerner of the thoughts and intents of the heart" (Hebrews 4:12). Also, God gives us this guarantee, "So shall My word be that goes forth from My mouth; It shall not return to Me void, But it shall accomplish what I please, And it shall prosper in the thing for which I sent it" (Isaiah 55:11). God's Word, shared prayerfully, will have His desired impact upon the heart of the unbeliever. It will help to convict them of their sins and point them to their need of a Savior. The following verses will give you a starting point. This list is by no means exhaustive:

Steps of God's Plan of Salvation

God Loves Us

✔ *John 3:16 "For God so loved the world that He gave His only begotten Son, that whoever believes in Him should not perish but have everlasting life."*

✔ *Romans 5:8 "But God demonstrates His own love toward us, in that while we were still sinners, Christ died for us."*

All Have Sinned

✔ *Romans 3:10 "As it is written: 'There is none righteous, no, not one;'"*

✔ *Romans 3:23 "for all have sinned and fall short of the glory of God,"*

JESUS DIED FOR OUR SINS

✔ *Romans 6:23* *"For the wages of sin is death, but the gift of God is eternal life in Christ Jesus our Lord."*

✔ *1 Corinthians 15:3-4* *"For I delivered to you first of all that which I also received: that Christ died for our sins according to the Scriptures, and that He was buried, and that He rose again the third day according to the Scriptures,"*

WE MAY BECOME SAVED RIGHT NOW

✔ *Revelation 3:20a* *"Behold, I stand at the door and knock. If anyone hears My voice and opens the door, I will come in to him . . ."*

✔ *Romans 10:13* *"For 'whoever calls on the name of the LORD shall be saved.'"*

✔ *John 1:12* *"But as many as received Him, to them He gave the right to become children of God, to those who believe in His name:"*

It is good to have a system for sharing the plan of salvation. Some people mark these verses in the Bible with a highlighter and then put red tabs on the pages so they are easier to find. Some will simply memorize the verses, and look them up as they go along. Others will have the verses typed on a sheet of paper (with page numbers where the verse is found) and put them inside the New Testament. Finally, some New Testaments can be purchased at bookstores that have the plan of salvation marked out. Whatever system you use, be sure you are prepared to flow as smoothly as possible through each step of the plan.

It is very important to review the plan of salvation with the unbeliever. Techniques can be helpful, but none is as good or powerful as the Word of God itself. The Word of God (coupled with the Holy Spirit) saves the soul, for "The law of the LORD is perfect, converting the soul" (Psalm 19:7).

> *having been born again, not of corruptible seed but incorruptible, through the word of God which lives and abides forever.*
> *1 Peter 1:23*

You will lead more people to trust Jesus Christ as Savior by simply reading these verses, than by your own knowledge, skills or abilities. Don't make it difficult. This is God's work, so why not let Him do it? Don't forget that Paul said, "a door was opened to me by the Lord" (2 Corinthians 2:12).

LEADING TO A DECISION

Next, it is very important that you lead the unbeliever ultimately to the point of decision. Knowledge is useless unless one actually receives Jesus Christ as their personal Savior. "You must be born again" (John 3:7). There are many phrases that you could say at this point, such as "Does this make sense to you?" Or "Would you like to receive God's free gift of eternal life?" If their response is positive, or when you sense that they understand their need for a Savior, you should encourage them to pray a "sinner's prayer" similar to the following:

Dear God, I realize that I have sinned against you and that I cannot save myself. I believe that Jesus Christ died on the cross and shed His blood to cleanse me from my sins. I believe He rose again, from the dead, that I might have eternal life. I ask You to forgive me of my sins and to come into my life. I pray this, sincerely. Jesus is Lord!

This is the point where many saints get weak in the knees. For some reason, we are bold about Christ until it gets to the actual point of praying for salvation. This must not be so. Eternity hangs in the balance. We need to increase our prayer and encourage them to make that decision for Christ.

Part of the problem, at this point, stems from an intense Spiritual battle. The devil won't give up without a fight. Recognize who the true enemy is:

For we do not wrestle against flesh and blood, but against principalities, against powers, against the rulers of the darkness of this age, against spiritual hosts of wickedness in the heavenly places.   *Ephesians 6:12*

This battle takes place in the mind, and the devil will try to sidetrack you at this point. The unbeliever may come out with any number of standard objections that the devil uses over and over again. In the next chapter, we will look at some of these objections and offer sound Biblical answers for them. Remember that we have the victory in Christ. Since this

Encourage them to make a decision for Christ

battle is fought in the mind, we have to take every thought captive (through prayer) to the obedience of Christ.

> *For though we walk in the flesh, we do not war according to the flesh. For the weapons of our warfare are not carnal but mighty in God for pulling down strongholds, casting down arguments and every high thing that exalts itself against the knowledge of God, bringing every thought into captivity to the obedience of Christ.*　　　*2 Corinthians 10:3-5*

Since this is a spiritual battle, it must be fought through prayer. Again, we must pray a prayer similar to the Colossians 4 prayer.

> *Walk in wisdom toward those who are outside, redeeming the time. Let your speech always be with grace, seasoned with salt, that you may know how you ought to answer each one.*
> *Colossians 4:5-6*

Then, by the leading of the Holy Spirit, who will "put My words in your mouth" (Jeremiah 1:9), we must step out in faith, answer their objections, and lead them back to a decision.

Since this is a step of faith, an often uncomfortable one, we must pray for boldness as Paul did:

> *praying always with all prayer and supplication in the Spirit . . . that utterance may be given to me, that I may open my mouth boldly to make known the mystery of the gospel . . . that in it I may speak boldly, as I ought to speak.*
> *Ephesians 6:18-20*

FINAL CONSIDERATIONS

When leading an unbeliever to make a decision for Christ, it is important that they understand what they are praying and that they are serious about their prayer. For only then, will they truly be saved. It is not a magical formula, but a repentant decision of the heart. Understand, of course, that we should never encourage a person to pray the sinner's prayer just for the sake of praying a prayer. This can cause more harm than good, by creating a false sense of security. Usually it is obvious, by the tone of their voice and their body language, whether or not they are serious about receiving Jesus Christ as their Savior.

Once the person prays to receive Jesus Christ as their personal Savior, it is important that you share the following "Assurance of Salvation" verses with them. Encourage them to read these verses regularly as this will solidify their decision for Christ. It will also help to quench the fiery darts of the devil who will most assuredly try to convince them that they are not really saved.

ASSURANCE OF SALVATION

✔ *1 John 5:13 "These things I have written to you who believe in the name of the Son of God, that you may know that you have eternal life, and that you may continue to believe in the name of the Son of God."*

✔ *Romans 10:9-10 "that if you confess with your mouth the Lord Jesus and believe in your heart that God has raised Him from the dead, you will be saved. For with the heart one believes unto righteousness, and with the mouth confession is made unto salvation."*

✔ *John 5:24 "Most assuredly, I say to you, he who hears My word and believes in Him who sent Me has everlasting life, and shall not come into judgment, but has passed from death into life."*

Connect the new believer with a Bible-believing church

Finally, it is important to connect the new believer with a local Bible-believing church, "for the equipping of the saints for the work of ministry" (Ephesians 4:12). This is a crucial time for them and they will need the fellowship, Bible study and prayer support that other Christian believers have to offer them.

not forsaking the assembling of ourselves together, as is the manner of some, but exhorting one another,   *Hebrews 10:25*

CHAPTER 7

ADDITIONAL WITNESSING HELPS

PROBING QUESTIONS

✔ Are you interested in spiritual things?

✔ Have you considered becoming a Christian?

✔ Who is Jesus?

✔ Have you come to a place in your spiritual walk that you know for certain you have eternal life, or is that something you would say you're still working on? [1]

✔ Suppose you were to die tonight and stand before God, and He were to ask you, "Why should I let you into My heaven?" What would you say? [2]

✔ If you were to die today, do you know for sure you would go to heaven?

✔ If you were wrong, would you want to know?

✔ What does this verse mean to you?

✔ Does this make sense to you?

✔ Would you like to receive God's free gift of eternal life?

These questions can be very helpful in personal witnessing. They are often effective in leading the conversation to the Lord Jesus Christ. However, do not rely on techniques apart from prayer and the Word of God. Let me give you an example.

I flew to Chicago on business and during the flight I prayed, "that God would open to us a door for the word, to speak the mystery of Christ" (Colossians 4:3). As I stepped off the plane, I had a strong sense that God would give me an opportunity to share Christ. It was 9:00 a.m. on a weekday and I had to take a 30-minute shuttle from O'Hare Airport to downtown Chicago. I had taken this trip several times and knew it would be a madhouse at that time of day.

A shuttle pulled up and I jumped on. The driver said, "We'll fill up (with passengers) and then head downtown." But no one else got on.

He waited a while and then said, "We'll go to the next stop, fill up, and then head downtown." So we did. But again, nobody got on. The driver was perplexed and said, "We have one more stop to pick up passengers. Then we'll go downtown." We went on to the next stop. Once again, no one got on. This was prime time on a weekday morning. Finally he said, "Well, I guess I can't hold you up any longer." And we headed for downtown Chicago.

It didn't take a rocket scientist to realize that God had opened a door for me to witness. I was very familiar with the question or technique, "If you were to die today, do you know for sure you would go to heaven?" I was about to ask that question, when the Holy Spirit impressed upon me, "Wait!" So I began to pray, "that God would open to us a door for the word, to speak the mystery of Christ" (Colossians 4:3).

As the driver pulled out on the expressway, a car passed him and honked his horn. The driver was very calm about the situation and it impressed me. So I said, "I appreciate the way you responded. Most drivers get very upset when someone honks at them." He humbly responded, "Why thank you, sir." This opened up a wonderful conversation, which quickly and naturally turned toward Jesus Christ. I was able to go through the entire plan of salvation with him, and he seemed genuinely interested.

I then asked him if I was bothering him and he said, "Oh no, *(Watch this!)* I have had many people try to shove Jesus down my throat, but you are the first one who has backed it up (with Scripture). It all makes sense to me."

Techniques must be used by the leading of the Holy Spirit

What if my opening line, before any conversation with him, had been, "If you were to die today, do you know for sure you would go to heaven?" Would I have been just one more person who

80

(in his opinion) was trying to shove Jesus down his throat? Probing questions and techniques are very helpful, but they must be used at the proper time, by the leading of the Holy Spirit.

BIBLE VERSES FOR DIFFERENT NEEDS

Following is a list of Bible verses for different needs that we face in life. As stated in Chapter 6, it is very important to use these when witnessing to unbelievers so they can see that God's Word was written to help them. This will draw them to want to read the Bible.

Situation	*Bible Verse*
Afraid	2 Timothy 1:7
	Hebrews 13:5-6
Angry	Ephesians 4:26-27
	James 1:19-20
Anxious	Matthew 6:19-34
	Philippians 4:6-7
Crisis	Matthew 6:23-34
	Hebrews 4:16

Situation	*Bible Verse*
Depressed	Romans 8:18, 31-39
	James 1:2-4
Discouraged	2 Corinthians 4:8-18
	Philippians 4:4-7
Doubting	Matthew 21:21-22
	Hebrews 4:1-3
Lonely	Hebrews 13:5-6
	John 15:4-11
Peace	John 14:1, 25-27
	Romans 5:1-5
Sick	James 5:13-16
	Romans 8:28, 38-39
Sorrowful	John 14
	2 Corinthians 1:3-4
Tempted	James 1:12-16
	1 Corinthians 10:12-14
	1 Peter 5:6-9
Weary	Matthew 11:28-30
	Galatians 6:9-10

HANDLING OBJECTIONS

The best way to handle any objection is to quote God's answer straight from the Bible. Following are Biblical responses for some questions or objections you may face. You may run into someone who says they don't believe the Bible. As stated in Chapter 4, don't let this deter you from sharing God's Word. The reason is found in Scripture itself:

> *For the word of God is living and powerful, and sharper than any two-edged sword, piercing even to the division of soul and spirit, and of joints and marrow, and is a discerner of the thoughts and intents of the heart.*   Hebrews 4:12

Please understand, I am not opposed to apologetics and other witnessing techniques. In fact, there is a plethora of these items on the market and good ones at that. However, my fear is that people will rely on their knowledge and abilities, rather than the Word and Spirit of God. Simply put, if God doesn't "open a door," no one will come to Christ.

The Word of God is our best defense when answering any question or objection. It will have an ongoing influence in the life of the unbeliever for years to come, even though it may not appear that way at first. God's Word will have a "haunting effect," so to speak, but in a very positive way.

One day a man was handing out tracts on a street corner. An angry unbeliever grabbed the tract and tore it into pieces. He threw it back at the Christian, along with some vocal obscenities, and stormed down the road. That night, when he was preparing for bed, he found a small piece of the tract that had been caught in his belt. The piece said simply, "and God said." "God said What?" he wondered. This haunted him for days. Finally, one day, he found that Christian and asked him for another one of those tracts. He found out what God had said and received Jesus Christ as Savior that day.

God's Word is the most powerful weapon on the face of the earth and is capable of winning this spiritual battle. Make no mistake about it. **This is a spiritual battle.**

Most objections, during personal witnessing, come straight from the enemy's camp.

For we do not wrestle against flesh and blood, but against principalities, against powers, against the rulers of the darkness of this age, against spiritual hosts of wickedness in the heavenly places.   *Ephesians 6:12*

Spend some time familiarizing yourself with the following concepts and Scripture verses. Jesus fought the devil using God's Word. Should we do any less? It is helpful to memorize key passages. You will then be better suited for the battle.

Be diligent to present yourself approved to God, a worker who does not need to be ashamed, rightly dividing the word of truth.   *2 Timothy 2:15*

Once you have become familiar with the Scriptures, the Holy Spirit will remind you of them at the proper time. We need to expect God to guide our conversation. After all, He has promised it in His Word:

"But the Helper, the Holy Spirit, whom the Father will send in My name, He will teach you all things, and bring to your remembrance all things that I said to you."   John 14:26

Can't I Be Good Enough To Get To Heaven?

✔ *Ephesians 2:8-9 "For by grace you have been saved through faith, and that not of yourselves; it is the gift of God, not of works, lest anyone should boast."*

✔ *Titus 3:5 "not by works of righteousness which we have done, but according to His mercy He saved us, through the washing of regeneration and renewing of the Holy Spirit,"*

✔ *Galatians 2:16 "knowing that a man is not justified by the works of the law but by faith in Jesus Christ, even we have believed in Christ Jesus, that we might be justified by faith in Christ and not by the works of the law; for by the works of the law no flesh shall be justified."*

I Am Not Ready To Become A Christian

✔ *2 Corinthians 6:2b* *"Behold, now is the accepted time; behold, now is the day of salvation."*

✔ *Hebrews 2:3a* *"how shall we escape if we neglect so great a salvation"*

✔ *Hebrews 3:15* *"while it is said: 'Today, if you will hear His voice, Do not harden your hearts as in the rebellion.'"*

✔ *Hebrews 9:27* *"And as it is appointed for men to die once, but after this the judgment,"*

What About Those Who Never Had a Chance to Hear?

✔ *Romans 1:18-20* *"For the wrath of God is revealed from heaven against all ungodliness and unrighteousness of men, who suppress the truth in unrighteousness, because what may be known of God is manifest in them, for God has shown it to them. For since the creation of the world His invisible attributes are clearly seen, being understood by the things that are made, even His eternal power and Godhead, so that they are without excuse,"*

HOW DO I KNOW THE BIBLE IS TRUE?
- or -
I DON'T BELIEVE IN THE BIBLE

✔ *2 Timothy 3:16* *"All Scripture is given by inspiration of God, and is profitable for doctrine, for reproof, for correction, for instruction in righteousness,"*

✔ *2 Peter 1:20-21* *"knowing this first, that no prophecy of Scripture is of any private interpretation, for prophecy never came by the will of man, but holy men of God spoke as they were moved by the Holy Spirit."*

✔ *1 Thessalonians 2:13* *"For this reason we also thank God without ceasing, because when you received the word of God which you heard from us, you welcomed it not as the word of men, but as it is in truth, the word of God, which also effectively works in you who believe."*

What About The Theory Of Evolution?

✔ *Genesis 1:1 "In the beginning God created the heavens and the earth."*

✔ *Genesis 1:26-27 "Then God said, 'Let Us make man in Our image, according to Our likeness; let them have dominion over the fish of the sea, over the birds of the air, and over the cattle, over all the earth and over every creeping thing that creeps on the earth.' So God created man in His own image; in the image of God He created him; male and female He created them."*

✔ *Jeremiah 1:5 "Before I formed you in the womb I knew you; Before you were born I sanctified you; I ordained you a prophet to the nations."*

✔ *John 1:1-3 "In the beginning was the Word, and the Word was with God, and the Word was God. He was in the beginning with God. All things were made through Him, and without Him nothing was made that was made."*

A LOVING GOD WON'T SEND ME TO HELL
- or -
I BELIEVE EVERYONE WILL GO TO HEAVEN

✔ *Revelation 20:10, 14-15* *"The devil, who deceived them, was cast into the lake of fire and brimstone where the beast and the false prophet are. And they will be tormented day and night forever and ever . . . Then Death and Hades were cast into the lake of fire. This is the second death. And anyone not found written in the Book of Life was cast into the lake of fire."*

✔ *Matthew 13:49-50* *"So it will be at the end of the age. The angels will come forth, separate the wicked from among the just, and cast them into the furnace of fire. There will be wailing and gnashing of teeth."*

✔ *Matthew 25:41, 46* *"Then He will also say to those on the left hand, 'Depart from Me, you cursed, into the everlasting fire prepared for the devil and his angels: . . .' And these will go away into everlasting punishment, but the righteous into eternal life."*

WHAT ABOUT ALL THE
HYPOCRITES IN THE CHURCH?

✔ *Romans 7:18-23* *"For I know that in me (that is, in my flesh) nothing good dwells; for to will is present with me, but how to perform what is good I do not find. For the good that I will to do, I do not do; but the evil I will not to do, that I practice. Now if I do what I will not to do, it is no longer I who do it, but sin that dwells in me. I find then a law, that evil is present with me, the one who wills to do good. For I delight in the law of God according to the inward man. But I see another law in my members, warring against the law of my mind, and bringing me into captivity to the law of sin which is in my members."*

✔ *Galatians 5:17* *"For the flesh lusts against the Spirit, and the Spirit against the flesh; and these are contrary to one another, so that you do not do the things that you wish."*

✔ *Jeremiah 17:9* *"The heart is deceitful above all things, And desperately wicked; Who can know it?"*

What About Other Religions?
- or -
Don't All Roads Lead to Heaven?

✔ *John 14:6 "Jesus said to him, 'I am the way, the truth, and the life. No one comes to the Father except through Me.'"*

✔ *Acts 4:12 "Nor is there salvation in any other, for there is no other name under heaven given among men by which we must be saved."*

✔ *John 3:36 "He who believes in the Son has everlasting life; and he who does not believe the Son shall not see life, but the wrath of God abides on him."*

What About Reincarnation?

✔ *Hebrews 9:27 "And as it is appointed for men to die once, but after this the judgment,"*

(1) D. James Kennedy, Evangelism Explosion (Tyndale House Publishers, 1996) page 75.

(2) Ibid., page 77.

CHAPTER 8

WRAPPING IT UP

The good news is that witnessing can be as natural as carrying on a conversation with a friend, when God is involved. It all starts when you memorize the Colossians 4 prayer. Pray this prayer daily, or even more often. God will begin to open doors and bring hungry hearts across your path. You can expect it, since this prayer is according to God's will. Keep in mind there is no magic in the words.

Witnessing is as natural as having a conversation with a friend

The key lies in your understanding of this prayer and your sincere intent on winning others to Christ. Try it for a while and see what God will do.

Continue earnestly in prayer, being vigilant in it with thanksgiving; meanwhile praying also for us, that God would open to us a door for the word, to speak the mystery of Christ, for which I am also in chains, that I may make it manifest, as I ought to speak. Walk in wisdom toward those who are outside, redeeming the time. Let your speech always be with grace, seasoned with salt, that you may know how you ought to answer each one. Colossians 4:2-6

The reason this prayer is so important is because the gospel is a mystery to the unbeliever. The devil has hidden it from their minds. Unless God reveals it to them, the unbeliever will remain hopelessly lost. But it is not God's will that any should perish, so there is hope for the unbeliever. God will reveal it to them in answer to our specific prayers and through the reading, or hearing, of His powerful Word.

We must study and memorize key passages in God's Word so that we are prepared for the spiritual battle that will ensue when we are involved in personal witnessing. Just like Jesus, we need to use the sword of the Spirit, which is the Word of God, when fighting this spiritual battle.

Finally, we need to step out in faith. We have to be willing to get out of the comfort zone. But when we do take that step of faith, we will miraculously find it is not as uncomfortable as we had feared. If we pray, and allow God to take the lead, He will. He will then prepare their hearts to receive the words that He will give us to share.

We will become effective in personal witnessing. God will use us to lead unbelievers to a saving knowledge of the Lord Jesus Christ. Then, we will truly experience, along with the apostle Paul, the *Secret to an Open Door.*

TAKING IT TO THE STREETS

A wise man once said that a good definition for the word "commitment" could be as follows: *"Commitment is the ability to carry out a worthy cause beyond the inspiration of the moment."* Clearly, saving people from a burning hell for all eternity is a worthy cause, and perhaps you are now inspired and desirous to join this cause. So what is needed next is to carry out this worthy cause. In all reality, many Christians want to bring people to Jesus, but the cares of this world encumber us to the point that we don't get involved. What is needed is an ongoing presence of mind, or consciousness of the need, to fulfill The Great Commission as stated in the following verses:

"Go into all the world and preach the gospel to every creature."   *Mark 16:15*

"Go therefore and make disciples of all the nations, baptizing them in the name of the Father and of the Son and of the Holy Spirit, teaching them to observe all things that I have commanded you; and lo, I am with you always, even to the end of the age." Amen.
                                        Matthew 28:19-20

Please notice that the first word in both of these commands of Jesus, is to "GO." Jesus has told us in no uncertain terms that we need to "GO" preach the gospel and make disciples. Here is where the rubber meets the road. When you are sitting at a red light and it turns green, you "GO." Therefore, I propose to everyone who reads this book, when you are driving and see a green light, that you pray for the lost. This will likely bring it to your mind several times a day. When you see a green light, pray for the lost! You might pray the Colossians 4 prayer. You might simply pray, "Save them Lord!" You might pray, "Give me an open door to share the gospel today." But when the light turns green, pray for the lost!

It is well documented that every great revival has been birthed out of prayer. What is needed is for thousands of Christians to pray regularly for the lost. In order for that to happen we need an ongoing consciousness of the need. The green traffic light can be the key to bring this to our mind on a regular basis. So remember, when the light turns green, pray for the lost! Then, look for the open door and walk through it by faith. *"Commitment is the ability to carry out a worthy cause beyond the inspiration of the moment."*

When the light turns green, pray for the lost!